A CENTURY *of*
BOSTON

The Guildhall became the town museum in 1929. St Mary's Guildhall was built in about 1450 and was occupied by the guild until it had to hand over its assets to the corporation in 1545. Thereafter the building was used as Town Hall, Banqueting Hall, Council Chamber, Courtroom and cells until the nineteenth century. Some of the Pilgrim Fathers were imprisoned in the cells before their epic voyage on the *Mayflower*.

A CENTURY *of* BOSTON

DAVID CUPPLEDITCH

WHSmith

First published in the United Kingdom in 2002 by
Sutton Publishing Limited exclusively for
WHSmith, Greenbridge Road, Swindon SN3 3LD

British Library Cataloguing in Publication Data
A catalogue record for this book is available from the British Library.

ISBN 0-7509-3103-5

Illustrations

Front endpaper: George Hackford's view of the Market Place in the late nineteenth century.
Back endpaper: HM Bark *Endeavour* arriving in Boston, Lincolnshire, 1997.
Half title page: Even in the 1950s there was quite a flotilla of small boats which plied their way up and down the Haven, but this could not compare with 1894 when there were fifty-eight smacks fishing solely for mussels and employing 140 men.
Title page: Boston dock at night.

For Alison

Typeset in 11/14pt Photina and produced by
Sutton Publishing Limited, Phoenix Mill,
Thrupp, Stroud, Gloucestershire GL5 2BU.
Printed and bound in England by
J.H. Haynes & Co. Ltd, Sparkford.

Contents

Boston Stump looking over the Fydell vaults.

Introduction

Boston's history is a tribute to its people. From the time St Botolph, patron saint of travellers and itinerants, founded his first monastery in 654 to the upheavals of the Danish invasion 200 years later and beyond, the town embraced an individual outlook on life which left the rest of England far behind. The Hanseatic League, a great trading organisation of the medieval and early modern periods, had warehouses overlooking the river and from its foundation in 1200 St Botolph's midsummer fair became one of the greatest trading events in northern Europe. Indeed, one could be mistaken for thinking this was the forerunner of the European Union.

But there were bad times as well as good. The area around the town was often beset with floods, and the dreaded plague wiped out about a third of the population in the fourteenth century. In 1287 a gang disguised as monks and canons set fire to three areas of the town at fair time and looted stalls and shops. Their leader, Robert Chamberlayne, was hanged but the rest of the gang escaped. Almost three centuries later in 1571 a momentous flood brought havoc to the east coast. Its events were described many years later by the Victorian poet Jean Ingelow in her 'High Tide on the Coast of Lincolnshire'.

Probably the most important historical landmark in the town's history came in 1607 when a group of English Separatists decided to set out from Boston to Holland in search of the freedom to follow their religious views. The men and women were betrayed by the ship's captain and tried at the Guildhall. Seven were imprisoned in the building's cells. These Separatists were eventually to join the epic voyage of the *Mayflower* from Plymouth to New England in 1620.

A total of thirteen vessels were chartered to carry the Separatists across the Atlantic. Two of the fleet sailed in advance and on 4 March 1630 four more ships made the legendary voyage, including the *Arbella*. She was named after Lady Arbella, wife of Isaac Johnson of Boston. The travellers reached the shores of America, the Massachusetts settlement of Trimountain was renamed Boston and thus began a mother-and-daughter relationship between the two Bostons which continues to this day. John Cotton (1585–1652), the vicar of St Botolph's, became the Pilgrims' spiritual leader and five governors of the state of Massachusetts came from Lincolnshire. When Joseph Kennedy (father of John F.) visited Boston in 1938 in his capacity as US ambassador to Britain he said the Puritans 'possessed courage, the urge for liberty and an appreciation of individual rights'.

Boston Stump and the statue of Herbert Ingram (1811–60), founder of the *Illustrated London News*. At the foot of his statue is a female figure pouring water from an urn to remind us that Ingram was responsible for Boston's first supply of piped water. He is remembered locally for this contribution rather than any success he enjoyed in journalism.

Boston's international influence was not confined to America. The Australian connection through George Bass, Joseph Banks and Matthew Flinders left the Eyre Peninsula in South Australia with a Point Boston, Boston Bay, Boston Island (opposite Port Lincoln) and a host of other Lincolnshire-inspired placenames. A plaque to their memory lies at the foot of the Stump.

The desire to go seafaring can only have stemmed from the confidence drummed into every Boston schoolboy from an early age. And Bostonians have made a significant impact closer to home too. In the early nineteenth century two enterprising foremen called Mr Clayton and Mr Shuttleworth gave up their jobs in the town and went to Lincoln to make their fortune. Their names have gone down in history for their pioneering genius in the field of engineering.

In the twentieth century many events shaped the town. Boston played an important role in both world wars and its magnificent parish church underwent vital restoration. One of the men who played an important part in town life during this period was Reuben Salter (1864–1958). He was a socialist at heart, a newsagent by trade (he had previously trained as a compositor for the *Boston*

The pulpit from which the Revd John Cotton preached. He was vicar of St Botolph's from 1612 to 1631. In 1856 American Bostonians restored a side chapel at the church which is known today as the Cotton Chapel.

The list of local seafaring men and explorers who made a great impact on Australia. The plaque is at the foot of the Stump.

Children from Kirton Primary School dressed as Separatists who later became known as the Pilgrim Fathers.

Guardian) and a Primitive Methodist by religion. He was mayor in 1929 and like Herbert Ingram before him he was concerned with providing quality drinking water for Boston. He was responsible for seeing the completion of the Fordington Water Scheme, which was eventually opened in 1951. Boston's water supply had greatly troubled Ingram a century before. Salter may have been a physically small man but he mixed with giants and earned a giant reputation. Dubbed 'Little Reuben Salter' by the press in Boston, Massachusetts, he was given a ticker-tape reception when he visited the city in 1930 and was met by Mayor Curly and William Randolph Hearst.

Changes came thick and fast through the twentieth century but towards the end of the 1970s great developments took place in Boston. In 1976 Princess Anne opened the new Pilgrim Hospital built by Trent Regional Health Authority at a cost of over £8 million, with 500 beds and accommodation for students and staff. In 1978 the John Adams Way was opened and the cattle and sheep pens in Bargate were cleared. Strait Bargate was pedestrianised and the highest ever flood level was recorded in the town – a mark at the foot of the Stump indicates the height of the waters.

These events, like thousands of others over the last 150 years, were recorded on film. And the photographs that accumulated down the decades have made this book possible. Many have come from the Boston Preservation Trust's collection, particularly an important album of images taken by local photographer George Hackford at the end of the nineteenth and beginning of the twentieth centuries. More recent scenes were captured by Derek Addy and Gary Atkinson, and their pictures also appear in the pages that follow. But what survives is only a fraction of the photographs taken to record the history of the town. A vast archive of glass negatives from Addy's firm – mostly dating from the 1920s and 1930s – was consigned to the bin, and some of Gary Atkinson's work was disposed of in the same way. Both collections were broken up because of a lack of space. Sadly, this author has heard the same tale many times before. However, it is to be hoped that the images which survive and have been brought together in these pages will jog a memory or two and even bring a smile to Bostonians young and old, giving a new perspective on the Capital of the Fens.

David Cuppleditch
August 2002

An Old Century &
A New Beginning

Although principally a portrait photographer, Luigi Cella also took a limited number of popular views. This is his image of the Stump.

This *carte-de-visite* of a Boston worthy was produced by Luigi Cella, whose studio was at 7a Wide Bargate. In Victorian times even the humblest families queued up to have a photograph taken.

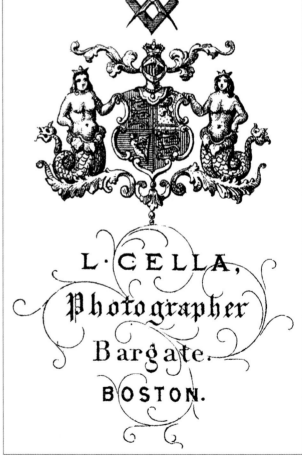

On the reverse of this *carte-de-visite* Cella has used a coat of arms very similar to that of the Boston Corporation, together with a masonic symbol. He lived at 9 Silver Street.

Other photographers included George Hackford (see below) and E.W. Peakome, who took over Cella's studio. Caleb C. Smith, who worked from 1 Norman Place, Lincoln, and 39 Wide Bargate, was another portrait photographer. This is his image of a Boston couple who have donned their best clothes for the occasion.

George Hackford's house, Church Close, with the man himself, George Hackford, in the topper in the foreground. One or two interested locals are standing there too. The house was renovated in 1999 and has adopted more of a lean than in Victorian times. The photograph was probably taken by Mrs Sarah Hackford (see overleaf).

Mrs Sarah Hackford, the photographer's wife.

Burton Hall on Wainfleet Road has an eerie, foreboding appearance. The ivy has been stripped off its walls since the time of this picture.

South Terrace, showing the Haven. Note the ferry in the foreground between Skirbeck Road and Pulvertoft Lane.

St Nicholas's Church, Skirbeck. The church was renovated in 1875 under the capable supervision of architect Sir Gilbert Scott.

Ingelow House, South Square, was the home where poet Jean Ingelow spent part of her childhood.

Boston Boys Grammar School. The pupils are posing in front of what was then the school hall and is now the library. One of the school's enduring traditions is the annual Beast Mart proclamation, made in the presence of the mayor, the council and the boys and masters of the school. The Beast Mart is still proclaimed in the Grammar School yard but it is many years since cattle were sold here.

West Skirbeck House, the residence of W. Garfitt, the banker whose premises were next to the Stump from 1864. Garfitt's bank is now occupied by Lloyds TSB.

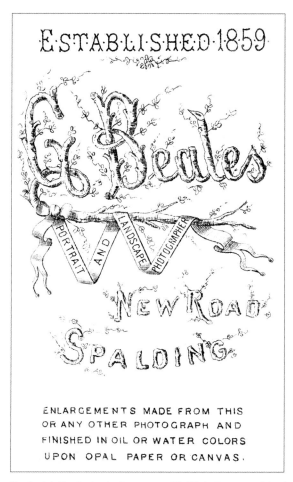

Frederick Beales's studio was at 31 High Street and he later opened a second at 2 West Street. His father, G. Beales of Spalding, was one of the earliest photographers in the county; he set up his business in 1859.

The Stump from Hussey Tower field. The Tower is all that remains of the once imposing Hussey Hall, demolished in the eighteenth century. It was named after Lord Hussey, Lord Lieutenant of Lincolnshire, who was beheaded at Lincoln in 1537 for failing to suppress the Lincolnshire Rising.

The Victorians put their stamp on everything with great conviction. Buildings in particular were built with a practical and solid look, as is clear from these desirable dwellings in Spilsby Road, Skirbeck.

The Priory, Frieston, was a good example of Victorian exuberance. Here the family have gathered outside to be photographed in front of their pride and joy. This picture came from the collection of the Venerable Archdeacon Edward Trollope and was taken by George Hackford.

During the Victorian period there was a revival of interest in the Gothic style. One of its chief proponents was architect Augustus Pugin, who designed the font at St Botolph's and the interior of the Houses of Parliament. The best Boston example of mock-Gothic architecture is the Sessions House, which is now the Magistrates Court. It was built in 1843 by architect Charles Kirk.

Before photography only prints such as this of the Market Place by Jabus Barwick (*c.* 1830) were available to the public.

Edwardian holidaymakers enjoying the fresh air and bathing facilities at Frieston Shore. The Marine Hotel is in the background. Omnibuses ran daily from Boston's railway station, White Horse Inn and Market Place. The two men with guns may have been enjoying shooting fowl, an activity for which this stretch of water was famous. Samphire grew all along this coast.

Victorian Bostonians put a great deal of emphasis on education and indeed the twentieth century benefited from their foresight. This is Mary Gee's school. She was the daughter of a banker whose business was next door to the White Hart Hotel. It was taken over by the Lincoln & Lindsey Bank and is now a branch of the HSBC.

Miss Blenkin's school. It was known as the Blue Girls' school because of the colour of the uniform. Blenkin Hall was named after her father, the Revd Blenkin, who was appointed Vicar of Boston in 1848.

These two views show the old vicarage and the new one built for the Revd Blenkin. Gone was the old Georgian building and in its place came a bold assurance of Victorian confidence.

The Stump from Packhorse Quay at the end of the nineteenth century. Compare this view with that on p. 78 taken by Derek Addy in 1959. Sir John Rennie's iron bridge (see p. 42) – in the middle distance – was demolished in 1913.

Skirbeck Quarter Oil Mill was built in 1870 to replace a windmill on this site beside the Black Sluice (left). It was constructed for J.C. Simonds & Son who imported seed for cattle cake and oil. Latterly, this building became a canning factory for Lin-Can. It was demolished in 1984 to make way for a supermarket.

An old clipper being towed into the Wash via the Haven by SS *Privateer*, *c*. 1880. Skirbeck church is on the right of the photograph.

Frampton Hall, photographed by George Hackford, *c*. 1880. At the time it was the home of Lieutenant Colonel Moores. The spire of Frampton church, dedicated to St Mary, is visible on the right.

Clearing the way for Boston's new port, 1883. The old Gallows Mills – Fishtoft, Skirbeck and the post mill – were demolished to make way for the new development. The designated area for the new port comprised just over 6 acres and building work cost £170,000.

This was Langrick Ferry just outside Boston, and it is possible to see the ferry being operated. One of the chief problems in the area was the traverse of the River Witham and the network of dykes that surrounded the town.

A young Arthur Towle (1885–1954) was given his first job at Shodfriars Theatre, sweeping the stage and selling programmes at *2d* a week. The performances there fuelled Arthur's imagination and ambition, and he appeared on stage in 1899 as a fourteen-year-old. He was to become the famous music-hall figure Old Mother Riley under his stage name of Arthur Lucan. The building had belonged to the Cabot family back in the sixteenth century.

Shodfriars Hall, photographed by George Hackford. It is easy to see the renovations of 1874. In 1929 it became a billiard hall.

This page and opposite: These two views of *c.* 1880, taken from the top of St Botolph's, show the Market Place with its statue of Herbert Ingram, founder of the *Illustrated London News*, in the foreground. Most notable are the shops that made way for the current Marks & Spencer building. In the picture opposite, beyond the Sessions House is the Centenary Chapel, and the Congregational Church, built in 1850, just to the right of it. The chapel burned down in 1909 (but was replaced in 1911) and the church was demolished in 1974 to make way for a car park.

The Boston & District Ploughing Society was founded in 1900, soon to be followed by the Boston & District Agricultural Union. To mark the ploughing society's inauguration, banners were put up around town. The one in the centre of the picture says 'He that tilleth shall have plenty', an adaptation of a quotation from Proverbs 28.

During the Ploughing Society inauguration celebrations most of the entrances to the town were festooned with flags. This is Bargate Bridge. Many of the buildings in this photograph were demolished when the inner relief road, John Adams Way, was constructed in the 1970s.

Bargate Green was decorated and the cannon given to the town in 1856 after the Crimean War were camouflaged with creepers.

A marquee was erected on the Green where visitors could eat lunch.
A selection of wooden gazebos were put on show, tempting ladies to buy one for their garden. These photographs were taken by Nainby of Alford.

A portrait of the Howe children in their Sunday best, 1902. Their father worked for Cheers men's outfitters, and the family left Boston in 1908 when their father was appointed manager of the Louth branch. Herbert Leslie Howe, known as Les, is on the right. He joined the railway, working as a goods clerk, but was a keen photographer. When he died in 1959 he left an invaluable record of life in northern Lincolnshire during the first half of the twentieth century.

Joseph Cooke was mayor from 1902 to 1904 and was known locally as the newspaper king. At various times he owned the *Spalding Guardian*, the *Doncaster Gazette*, the *Sheffield Independent*, the *Grantham Times* and, briefly, the *Louth Times*. His flagship, however, was the *Boston Guardian*.

On 16 June 1904 the Municipal Buildings in West Street were opened under the watchful eye of the mayor, Alderman Joseph Cooke. One of the main interior features of the building is this magnificent fireplace with the Boston coat of arms emblazoned on it. It is still in the Council Chamber today.

This was the view from the churchyard, looking down the Witham, before the Edwardian developers built on the other side.

The Wesleyan Centenary Methodist Chapel in Red Lion Street caught fire on 24 June 1909. It was a terrible blaze which gutted the whole building and meant it had to be demolished.

The new Wesleyan Chapel (also known as the Centenary Chapel) was opened in 1911. Designed by Messrs Gordon and Gunton of London, it was more elaborate than its predecessor.

Fred McGuire, fen ice-skating champion, 1910. In the days before the First World War the Witham often froze over and ice-skating competitions were held. McGuire later kept the Axe & Cleaver pub in West Street.

Flags, banners and bunting marked the coronation of George V and Queen Mary in 1911. This is the new post office, opened in 1907, with postmen and locals lined up to have their photograph taken.

Telegrams :
Hutson, Ironmongers, Boston

HUTSON BROS.

Telephone :
No. 107.

FURNISHING & BUILDERS' IRONMONGERS.

Hot Water Engineers, Plumbers and Gasfitters.

Large stock of Kitchen Ranges, Room Grates & Mantels to select from.

Tennis Rackets, Croquet Sets, Golf Clubs and Balls always in stock.

11 Wide Bargate - - Boston

Hutson Bros, 1912. There was clearly a call for tennis rackets, croquet sets and golf equipment in Boston at this time, together with a range of merchandise more appropriate for an ironmongers.

Sutcliffe & Co., steamship owners and shipbrokers, 32 Market Place, 1912.

Sir John Rennie's iron bridge stood over the Witham for about 100 years but was condemned in 1912. This is the new bridge under construction in 1913, and the photograph below shows the old bridge.

The lock-up was squeezed between the old town bridge and the Corporation Buildings. It was demolished when the iron bridge was taken down and used to house a nightwatchman whose job it was to keep an eye on the bridge and the river. When this photograph was taken it was being used as a tobacconists.

A temporary wooden structure for pedestrians was erected while Rennie's old bridge was being dismantled and Webster's new one erected. It looks very like the original wooden bridge that stood here before 1807.

This group of men helped to unload the iron work for the new bridge in the railway goods yard. Mr G. Booth is third from right, with Mr A. Shepherd next to him. The wheel at the bottom of the photograph is a piece of scrap from one of the lamp standards on Rennie's town bridge.

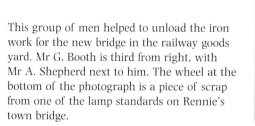

One of the early casualties of the First World War was the little tug SS *Privateer*. This paddle-steamer had been crucial to the work of dismantling Rennie's iron bridge and used to ferry day-trippers to Skegness and around the Wash. She was sunk off the coast of France in 1914.

Well water became contaminated and there was a risk to the town's health in 1914. Fearing a repeat of the 1905 typhoid epidemic in Lincoln, Boston Borough Council advised everyone to boil drinking water, and brought in barrels from outside the town.

War & Peace

During the First World War Frank Whitwork Dennis (1878–1969) bought the Peacock & Royal Hotel in the Market Place for women landworkers to use as a hostel. He is pictured here outside Frampton Hall, which he purchased in 1915. It is currently the home of Quentin Davies, MP for Stamford and Spalding.

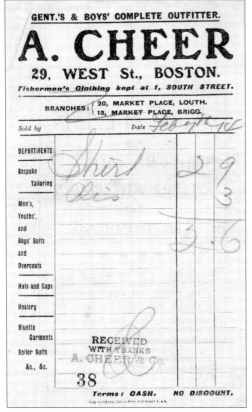

Lieutenant Oswald Giles collecting a batch of recruits, Market Place, 8 September 1914. War had been declared on 4 August; Lord Kitchener's pointing finger with the words 'Your Country Needs You' became a familiar slogan.

A shirt cost *2s 9d* in 1914 and staff discount was *3d*. When the war ended, inflation was soon to follow.

Charles Hardy, the founder of Hardy and Collins, farmed extensively in the Boston era. This family photograph was taken in 1921. Back row, left to right: Lilian Craven, Frank Hardy, Florence Tunnard, George Hardy, Doris Marjason, William Hardy, Ethel Wright, Frederick Hardy, Richard Hardy and Edith Neal. Front row: Harriet Craven, Charles Hardy (the Boss), Mrs Charles Hardy and Maud Grant.

Sam Leggate of Station Road, Sibsey, 1926. Sam was a familiar sight around Boston on his veteran cycle

This typical family from Frampton tried to eke out a living, growing produce to supplement their income, 1926.

The Wander & Addy Orchestra playing in the Assembly Rooms, *c.* 1926. The lighting was still gas-powered – the Assembly Rooms had no electricity at this time. Sid 'Rudy' Addy is on the extreme left and Fred Addy is second from right with the banjo. George 'Jazzy' Wander is at the piano.

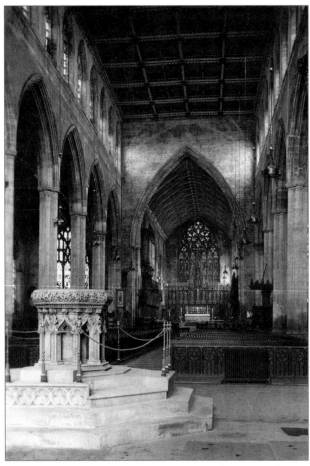

The restoration of St Botolph's began with a new roof, the original being badly infested with death-watch beetle. By the time this photograph was taken in 1923 the arched ceiling had been removed. Clearly visible in the foreground is the font designed by Augustus Pugin in 1853.

George Addy with camera poised, 1928. Known as Fred, he purchased Luigi Cella's old studio at 7a Wide Bargate before moving to no. 9 in 1925.

This was Addy's shop illuminated by the relatively new electric light at carnival time. It is easy to see why it was nicknamed 'the electric studio'. The studio had its own generator.

Arthur (Towle) Lucan's big break occurred on 8 May 1934 when he appeared in *Bridgette's Night Out* with Kitty McShane (his wife) at the London Palladium in front of King George V and Queen Mary. After this he was able to add 'The Royal Command Favourites' to his posters, and his character Old Mother Riley caught the public's imagination. He started making films in 1935 and became one of Britain's most popular stars during the war years. His stage and screen daughter was played by Kitty McShane (1898–1964). They were married in 1913 and their off-stage rows were legendary. It is only recently that a street has been named after him in Sibsey.

In 1933 the Lincolnshire Show was held at Boston. This was Hutson's stand with Geoff Hutson standing on the right with hand on hip. Displayed are the mangles, hoovers, wringer-washtubs, deck chairs, paraffin cookers and Robin Hood coke boilers available at that time. Geoff Hutson was a keen sportsman and a radio ham (call sign G6GH). During the Second World War he was stationed at Honington, near Grantham, while his uncle Bert and grandfather ran the shop.

The US Ambassador Joseph Kennedy signs the register on the occasion of the presentation of the American contribution towards the cost of restoring St Botolph's, 1932. Looking on is Canon A.M. Cook, vicar from 1931 to 1946, who penned numerous publications, and even when he was appointed sub-dean at Lincoln Cathedral did not forget his ties with Boston. It was architect Sir Charles Nicholson's report on the state of St Botolph's in general and the Stump in particular that prompted the massive fund-raising exercise. The people of Boston, Massachusetts, gave £11,000 (a huge sum in the 1930s), mainly thanks to the good offices of Allan Forbes.

In 1933 the Bishop of Rhode Island gave the address at the opening of the iron gates in the screen that commemorates the restoration of the tower.

The Red Lion in Strait Bargate, 1936. Originally this was an important coaching inn and then with the advent of the railway in 1848 a taxi service ferried guests between the Red Lion and the station, followed by omnibuses in 1894. The hotel closed in 1962 and Woolworth's was built on its site.

Market Place, 1937. The car in the foreground is a 1936 Ford Eight and next to it a Morris Ten. Soulby's Ales (its sign is on the Rum Puncheon) came from the brewery in nearby Alford.

George Hackford's view of the Market Place was taken nearly sixty years earlier than the one above and shows there had been little change in the intervening years, although the names on the shopfronts had altered by 1937.

Fydell House, 1938. The house was built in 1726 and acquired by William Fydell, a prosperous wine merchant and mayor of Boston. In 1813, when the last of the Fydells died, it was occupied by a relative, Henry Rogers, who was the town clerk. It was purchased by the Boston Preservation Trust in 1935 to rescue it from demolition. The American Room opened in 1938 for the use of visitors from the USA. Fydell House is currently the home of Pilgrim College, an offshoot of Nottingham University.

This was the back of Fydell House in Victorian times. Over the years creeper had eaten into the brickwork and the building looked very forlorn.

On 18 July 1838 Joseph Kennedy, the US ambassador, came back to Boston to open the reading room for American visitors at Fydell House. Left to right: T.E. Dennis, Sir Frederick Whyte, Joseph Kennedy, the Earl of Ancaster and Canon A.M. Cook. Joseph Kennedy's sons John Fitzgerald, Robert and Edward were to play an important role in twentieth-century American politics.

Doughty Quay and High Street with Burton Allton's warehouse in the foreground, 1937. Latterly this building was used by Van Smirren's but it is now a private house.

The Second World War
& Beyond

After the 1930 visit of Mayor Reuben Salter to Boston, Massachusetts, an annual pilgrimage took place on the third Sunday in July of Americans to Boston, Lincolnshire. In the early days of the Second World War this was carried out by a representative of the American Embassy but in 1943 over 100 officers, nurses and men from the American armed forces brought a silken Stars and Stripes to be hung in Boston Council Chamber.

On Good Friday 1940 one of a string of bombs fell in Wide Bargate just outside Cammack's department store. Fortunately it did not explode. In 1919 Francis Cammack set up his business in the town, moving to its present location in 1932. At the outbreak of the Second World War Mr F.A. Cammack retired and the firm carried on as a partnership of his three sons, Sydney, Frank and Kenneth.

To aid the war effort and raise morale the Duchess of Gloucester visited the town. She was met by Mayor John Grainge Wrigley and his wife Emma. John Wrigley was the potato buyer for the Co-operative Wholesale Society based in Boston. He was also the first Conservative mayor to be sponsored by the unions.

She also inspected that unsung army, the Royal Observer Corps, which was comprised largely of volunteers considered unfit or too old for active service, in Central Park.

The Duchess continued to inspect a company of girl guides. Visible just behind her is C.L. Hoffrock Griffiths, the Town Clerk, who was a founding member of Blackfriars Theatre and Chairman of the Boston Lawn Tennis Club.

The turning-point in the war came in 1943, after the blitz, the Battle of the Atlantic and the ignominy of Dunkirk. Lincolnshire played its part with the mobilisation of hundreds of airfields scattered across the county. In 1937 work had begun on building an aerodrome at Coningsby. At the outbreak of war it was still under construction and did not become operational until 4 November 1940. Equipped with Manchesters it took part in the famous Thousand Bomber raid on Cologne in May 1942. From September 1942 to August 1943 hard runways were laid. Lancasters flew from Coningsby till the end of the war, and then Lincolns. In 1954 an expansion took place at Coningsby which included an extension of the runways. The station closed for flying for a year until the work was finally completed in 1956. Boston had built up a special rapport with RAF Coningsby and bestowed the Freedom of the town on the RAF base in September 1963. The county's part in the air battles of the Second World War is commemorated at the Lincolnshire Aviation Heritage Centre, East Kirkby. This is the centre's Lancaster *Just Jane* which has been restored to full ground-running condition by Fred and Harold Panton and their dedicated team. Fred and Harold had an elder brother called Christopher who was a flight engineer in a Halifax that was shot down on the Nuremberg raid in March 1944. They bought *Just Jane*, serial number NX 611, when she came up for sale in 1983 and restored her in memory of their brother and as a tribute to the Royal Air Force, and the aircraft and men of Bomber Command.

NEWS CHRONICLE, Tuesday, May 8, 1945

VICTORY ISSUE
May 8, 1945

News Chronicle

No. 30,881 · TUESDAY, MAY 8, 1945 · · · ONE PENNY

TODAY IS V DAY

Churchill speaks at 3 p.m., the King at 9; Today and tomorrow are national holidays

TODAY is V Day and a public holiday.

Tomorrow is V Day plus one and is also a public holiday.

This was announced last night in the following official statement:

"It is understood that in accordance with arrangements between the three Great Powers an official announcement will be broadcast by the Prime Minister at three o'clock tomorrow afternoon, May 8.

"In view of this fact, tomorrow, Tuesday, will be treated as Victory in Europe Day and will be regarded as a holiday. The day following, May 9, will also be a holiday.

"His Majesty the King will broadcast to the peoples of the British Empire and Commonwealth tomorrow at 9 p.m.

"Parliament will meet at the usual time tomorrow."

It may be that shortly after the Premier's announcement the Commons will go in procession to St. Margaret's to give thanks, headed by the Speaker, Col. Clifton Brown, who will be preceded by the Mace carried by Sir Charles Howard. The Lords will go to Westminster Abbey.

The complete and unconditional surrender of Germany was first announced to the world at 2.9 yesterday afternoon by the Germans themselves.

Broadcasting then, von Krosigk, the Foreign Minister, said: "The High Command of the armed forces, at the order of Grand Admiral Doenitz, has today declared the unconditional surrender of all fighting German troops."

The surrender had been signed at 2.41 a.m., in the small red schoolhouse near Rheims which Gen. Eisenhower uses as his headquarters.

There were three other broadcasts during the day:

The announcement by Doenitz that on May 4 he had ordered all U-boats to return to their bases;

The declaration by the German-controlled Prague station that the Germans there would ignore the surrender; and

A Danish report that the Germans in Norway had capitulated, to which the Swedes added that an Allied fleet of 48 ships was off Oslo Fiord.

FULL SURRENDER SIGNED IN A SCHOOLROOM

RHEIMS, Monday.

AT 2.41 a.m. today Col.-Gen. Gustav Jodl, German Chief of Staff, signed the unconditional surrender of Germany in the little red schoolhouse which is Gen. Eisenhower's H.Q.

Gen. Eisenhower was not present. For Britain and the U.S. Gen. Bedell-Smith signed the surrender document; Gen. Ivan Suslaparov signed for the Soviet Union and Gen. Francois Sevez for France.

The German emissaries were repeatedly asked: "Do you understand the significance of the seriousness of the terms?" The Germans replied that they did.

LATE NEWS

BLACK-OUT IN NORWAY FINISHES

Blackout for the whole of Norway discontinued from last night, Oslo radio announced.

News Chronicle front page.

There were VE Day celebrations in the Market Place and artist H. Kemp managed to capture them on canvas. Such was the euphoria at the end of hostilities in Europe that practically the entire town turned out to celebrate the momentous occasion.

Arthur Lucan is seen here starring opposite Bela Lugosi in the 1952 film *Old Mother Riley Meets the Vampire*. Arthur Lucan died in 1954 while performing at the Tivoli Theatre, Hull. Despite commanding £1,000 a week in the 1930s and grossing a huge amount from his films, Lucan died penniless.

During the '50s there were two cinemas in Boston, the Regal in West Street and the Odeon in South Square. The Regal has since been converted into a shopping complex and the Odeon was demolished in 1999. Cinema-goers now choose between the five-screen West End multiplex in West Street and the Lawn cinema in Mo Brader's back garden in Wyberton (capacity: 5 persons).

Boston, 1951. The old gasometers have been removed since this picture was taken but the frontage of the old Union Workhouse on Skirbeck Road has recently been renovated.

In 1953, the year of Queen Elizabeth II's coronation, the Maud Foster windmill was restored. It was built for Thomas and Isaac Reckitt (their name retained in the company Reckitt & Colman) in 1819 and last operated in 1942. This photograph was taken by the late Hugh Martineau who did much work for *Lincolnshire Life* magazine.

Central Park, 1954. After the upheavals of the Second World War, Britain looked to more genteel activities and recreation. What could be more relaxing than watching cricket on a fine summer's day? Central Park was opened to the public in 1932. Before that it was known as Oldrid's Park, as in the well-known store.

The port of Boston, 1955. Imported timber has arrived here since the port was opened in 1884. In medieval times wine also arrived here and in the year 1301 alone 1½ million gallons passed through the quayside.

Bostonians have always been known for their ingenuity but Babycherry, produced in the town, did not catch on. However, its rival Babycham enjoyed huge success in the '60s.

In the 1950s the public could walk down to the dock and watch the ships being loaded and unloaded. The coal hoists have since been removed. The picture above was taken in about 1958, the one below in about 1955.

A lorry owned by A. Healey & Son, Surfleet, 1958. The days of the old horse and cart had come to an end. Incidentally the idea of Smash, the 'instant mashed potato', was talked about in Boston long before the packets reached the supermarket shelves.

A group of lads pose for a casual picture, 1957. On the left is Barry Spikings who produced the film *The Deer Hunter* with Robert De Niro in the leading role. This Bostonian was educated at the grammar school, and started work on the *Boston Standard*. He left to join *Farmer's Weekly*, before entering the world of films, and is now responsible for Castle Rock, one of the main film companies in the States. He lives in Malibu. In the middle is Roger Langley and on the right is *Boston Standard* photographer Gary Atkinson, who took many of the images in this book.

We can now look back on the '50s with a sense of nostalgia; although life was hard, it was less complicated than today. There is a timeless quality to this picture of harvesting in Farmer Hardy's fields in 1956, although even then Boston Crop Sprayers were encouraging the use of Runcatex to kill cleavers and chickweed and Mecpa Special for all-round weed control. The age of pesticides was already with us.

This page and opposite: Sailing up and down the Witham during Boston Regatta, 1957 – what an idyllic pursuit. What amuses the author is the captain with his brew-up – an essential for any seafaring cruise! In the snapshots opposite a picnic on the bank while watching the boats is hard to beat. There is even a photographer ready to capture the scene – but I'm not sure the rifle is really necessary. (See the gundog at the foot of the picture.)

In June 1958 Boston was twinned with Laval, the capital of the French *département* of Mayenne. This official photograph of the ceremony shows Boston's mayor, Cyril Valentine (second left) with his counterpart Monsieur le Docteur de Basser (wearing a sash around his midriff). The ceremony took place in the *hôtel de ville* at Laval. Boston's town clerk, Hoffrock Griffiths, is on the extreme left.

This view of Packhorse Quay in 1959 shows how little some parts of Boston have changed. Waite's warehouse on the right (later Sinclair's) was to be demolished in 1963.

From Austerity to Affluence

On 19 November 1964 David Jacobs, presenter of the popular television programme *Juke Box Jury*, came to open the new Starlight Rooms at the Gliderdrome. The venue had a revolving stage! Mayor Bert Eyre is holding the drumsticks. The decision to build the Starlight Rooms at a cost of £60,000 was a brave one.

Frieston Shore, 1960. As it said in *White's Lincolnshire* of 1892, 'Frieston Shore has a number of lodging houses and two good hotels pleasantly situated near the sea bank. It is resorted to in summer by the people of Boston.' Both Frieston Shore and Scrane End were popular hamlets.

Bostonian David Bolland (far right) with a group of young socialists at their Skegness conference in July 1961. Centre stage is Prime Minister Harold Wilson in typical pipe-in-mouth pose, while Barbara Castle stands in the foreground with handbag – an accessory Margaret Thatcher was later to adopt.

A pleasure boat travels the River Witham as a train crosses the Grand Sluice railway bridge, 1961. The bridge was built in 1885 to replace a timber one of 1848.

Of all the pictures in this book, this one amuses the author most. It was taken during the 1962 regatta and the gentleman in the white coat is carefully demonstrating the advantages of using oxyacetylene while smoking!

Crews from Boston Rowing Club warm up for their race, 1962. Although the regatta was no longer held on the same grand scale as in Edwardian times, there was still an enthusiastic core of oarsmen.

Another crew – slightly younger – ready for the off.

The boat in the foreground is called *Merrydown*. Meanwhile the two crews in the background battle it out.

Businesses come and go. All these shops have changed hands since these photographs were taken in 1962. Maypole's grocery store, Walter Woodthorpe's coal merchants, Atkinson's women's clothing store and the café above the Home & Colonial have all disappeared, together with Blaskey's paint and wallpaper shop and Reynolds's grocery store. Even Harlow's pork butchers has gone, and the Benefit Shoe Store has been replaced by the Edinburgh Woollen Mill.

Boston's premier hotel was the old Peacock & Royal at the south end of Market Place. It finally closed its doors in 1963 to make way for a branch of Boots the Chemist. In 1891 Thomas Towle (father of Old Mother Riley) was given a job there as head groom on 16s a week.

The Assembly Rooms surrounded in scaffolding as a new coat of paint was applied, 1962. The Five Lamps, a local landmark, were erected in 1927 with the coming of electricity. It replaced the original gas-lit version presented to the town by Henry Rogers, town clerk.

The old Rum Puncheon, seen here in 1962, is now Martha's Vineyard. On this site had stood the house where John Foxe (1517–87) was born. His famous *Book of Martyrs* was published in Latin in 1558, with the English version appearing in 1563. This Protestant clergyman had much influence in the English Reformation.

Broughton's newsagents is Captain Cod's fish and chip shop. Broughton's used to sell Dinky Toys, Matchbox models and Meccano.

The twist swept Britain in 1962. These dancers were twisting the night away at the Glider. Local bands played here regularly and Joe Loss appeared occasionally, but as the Glider gained popularity it began to attract stars including Joe Brown & The Bruvvers and Emile Ford & The Checkmates. Originally the Glider had been a skating rink owned by the Malkinson family. The Malkinsons saw the potential of turning the Gliderdrome into a pop venue where youngsters could dance and hear the latest groups.

On 21 November 1964 The Animals, featuring Eric Burdon, performed at the Starlight Rooms. They were the first group to appear at the venue, the first in a long line of musicians that would read like a Who's Who of pop and included Tom Jones, the Walker Brothers, The Kinks, Billy Fury, The Hollies and Manfred Mann.

Among the girls who appeared at the Starlight Rooms were Lulu, Cathy McGowan and Brenda Lee. On 19 November 1964 Heinz Burt, the blond bombshell, and his backing group The Tornadoes were the star attraction. His hit 'Telstar' was Margaret Thatcher's favourite record. He died in obscurity in Southampton on 9 April 2000.

On 1 May 1965 P.J. Proby appeared at the Starlight Rooms in front of a packed audience and wearing his famous velvet trousers. The hysteria he generated is clear. A young Ted Eaglen, bouncer, is trying to keep back the crowds!

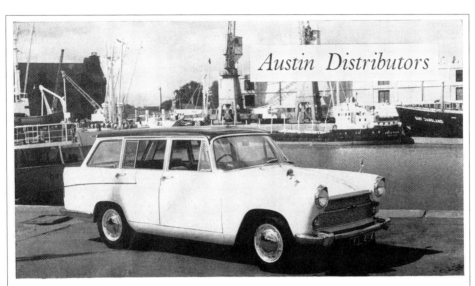

The dock served as a backdrop to this 1962 advert for R.M. Wright.

AUSTIN A 60 ESTATE CAR (£829 5s. 5d. incl. P.T.)

R. M. Wright (Boston) Ltd

**RILEY
AUSTIN - HEALEY**

WIDE BARGATE, BOSTON.

TELEPHONE 4404

On the far right are photographers Sid Phillipson and Derek Addy. The gentleman in the centre wearing a morning coat is Charles Sinclair from the firm Sinclair, Seed & Corn Merchants. The picture was taken in 1965.

The Wormgate Inn on the left, Wormgate, 1966. This pub is long gone but Blenkin Hall (right), named after the Revd Blenkin (see p. 28), still stands and is used as a Church House. The name Wormgate derives from the Anglo-Saxon 'wyrm' gate.

Boston United's army of devoted fans photographed on 28 October 1967 during a match against Bedford. Note the number of cloth caps still being worn in the 1960s.

Proudly raising their United scarves and Union flags, fans chant their approval in the photograph below and read all about their favourite players in the one above. Note the caricatures of footballing heroes in the *Boston Standard*.

The match between United and York City on 18 December 1970 was full of incident. Supporters were crammed into the stand in the background. Football has been played at the York Street stadium since the late 1800s. Originally there were two clubs in the town – Boston Town and the Boston Swifts. After the First World War the Swifts ceased playing. Boston United came into being in 1934.

Throughout the 1970s Britain was plagued with strikes. The public never knew from one week to the next where the following strike was coming from. On 13 February 1974 Boston Docks came to a standstill. In the photo above ships stand idle while in that below the NUM picket line enjoy their cuppa. In certain parts of the country picket lines were not tolerated with such good humour and violence often broke out.

On 20 June 1971 the Most Reverend and Right Honourable Arthur Ramsey, Archbishop of Canterbury, visited the town and preached at St Botolph's. Remembering happy times when he was a young curate-lecturer at the Stump between 1937 and 1939, he was photographed with members of the clergy and choir to mark the event. Mark Spurrell, who wrote *The Puritan Town of Boston*, is seated far right. He was appointed lecturer of St Botolph's in 1965 and went on to become vicar of Stow, Lincolnshire.

T-Rex were one of the last bands to play at the Gliderdrome before it was forced to close because of vandalism in September 1973. The group appeared on 15 January 1972, led by the ill-fated Marc Bolan who was to die so tragically in a car accident in 1978.

Artist Charles Whittaker mid-sketch in the park, 1972. Whittaker was noted for his watercolours. He exhibited at the Royal Watercolour Society on one or two occasions. Although not a native by birth, Boston became his adopted home.

The many changes that took place in the town in the '70s included clearing away the sheep and cattle pens in Bargate. The May Fair had once been held here and up to 30,000 sheep would exchange hands on a single day. Like so many other Lincolnshire towns that lost their cattle markets it was a sign of the changes in traditional farming.

All the changes meant that nostalgic views like this Christmas card scene would be a thing of the past.

**BARGATE
BOSTON
2454**

ADDYS of BOSTON

Designed their new shop to include extended
Galleries and Hi-Fi Showrooms

Addy's photography shop, seen here in 1972, also sold fine art
and hi-fi equipment. It was known as diversification!

A slim Elton John appeared at the Gliderdrome in 1973. It was
the perfect opportunity to meet his lyricist, the Owersby-born
and Market Rasen-educated Bernie Taupin who lived at Tealby.
This was before he moved to the USA.

During the '60s Boston was plagued by traffic trying to get through the town. A bypass had been under discussion for many years and eventually John Adams Way was constructed to cut through the town, and now passes on the extreme right of this picture, taken in about 1970.

This page and opposite: Like so many other Lincolnshire towns Boston has its fair share of characters. These locals were captured on film by Derek Addy on a May market day in 1976. One surprising addition recently has been the disgraced Jeffrey Archer – now an inmate of North Sea Prison Camp, and known as prisoner No. FS8282.

Someone once said of Boston, 'It's all dykes, daffs and windmills.' This flower arrangement created for Queen Elizabeth II's silver jubilee in 1977 certainly reinforced the statement.

This *c.* 1975 view of Strait Bargate shows Hutson's hardware shop on the left with Addy's photography shop next door.

This vehicle got stuck in Strait Bargate in 1978. Boston's narrow streets were certainly not designed to take this type of carriage.

It wasn't the accident pictured above that caused Strait Bargate to be pedestrianised, but rather an accumulation of incidents. Pedestrianisation had yet to happen when this 1960s picture, which clearly shows the old W.H. Smith's frontage, was taken.

Looking the other way up Strait Bargate with Oldrid's store on the right. Strait Bargate had been pedestrianised by the time this photograph was taken in about 1980.

A Thoroughly Modern Town

On 24 September 1989 the Geoff Moulder Leisure Pool in Rowley Road opened, drastically improving swimming and keep fit facilities. This is Mr Moulder, who was mayor that year, receiving a commemorative book to mark the occasion.

Packhorse Quay is on the left and Van Smirren's old premises are in the middle distance, 1983. On the left is Lincoln's Warehouse, now the Sam Newsom Music Centre. Before Boston Port came into existence in 1884 Packhorse Quay was a hive of activity.

In January 1990 the Port of Boston was privatised and was bought by a consortium including Richard Budge and James Sutcliffe for £1 million.

On behalf of HMS *Cottesmore* and her crew, Prince Andrew, Duke of York accepted an illuminated scroll recording the granting of the freedom of Boston to the vessel and her men in 1994. Mayor Keith Dobson JP presented the honour to the prince. Just visible to the right of the mayor is his officer Horace Wright wearing his ceremonial top hat. The mayor of Boston is also Admiral of the Wash so when Prince Andrew arrived on *Cottesmore* he had to report directly to the mayor. HMS *Cottesmore* was built in Scotland and launched by Lady Buchanan on 9 February 1982. She is the second ship to bear the name and is a Hunt class mine countermeasures vessel.

Many Boston people give their time to charitable causes. This is Stanley ('Stan') Meeds receiving the Voluntary Medical Service Medal from the Red Cross on 1 January 1994.

Princess Anne visited the town in 1995 to mark the 450th anniversary of Boston's incorporation as a borough. She was accompanied by Mayor Judy Cammack and crowds turned out to catch a glimpse of her.

Barry Spikings agreed to officiate at Boston Grammar School's prize-giving in 1995. On the extreme left is Mrs Spikings and on the right is Barry's father Maurice with Mayor Judy Cammack.

On Saturday 23 March 1996 an event was held in St Botolph's Church to mark the centenary of the Mothers' Union. Left to right: Dick Leafe, Michelle Dalliston, Fred Moss, Pearl Danby, -?-, Sister Cath Bailey of the Church Army, -?-, -?-, Bishop Frank Sargeant (one of Boston's most distinguished sons), Judy Cammack, Revd Chris Dalliston, Revd Bill Page (Vicar of Sibsey), -?-, -?-, Eileen Hewitt and Joan Moss.

Chirpy television cleric Roger Royle in the Centenary Chapel, Red Lion Street, late 1990s. Left to right: Revd John Kennedy, Charlie White, Margaret Hardy, Roger Royle, Mildred Chapman, Revd Douglas Allan and Revd Albert Harbey. Those holding certificates had just been awarded their long-service preaching awards.

Celebrating the centenary of Conway Preparatory School in 1996, pupils dressed in boaters, bow ties and waistcoats to embody an earlier age.

Today's photographs are tomorrow's history. These are the pupils of Butterwick School enjoying the panto *Aladdin*, late 1990s.

A race for weird and wonderful water craft at Nunn's Bridge, Fishtoft. This miscellaneous collection of vessels can include Viking longboats, cars and various Heath Robinson-type rafts. The team from the Bull and Dog pub, Frieston, have always done well in this annual race which started in 1994.

HM Bark *Endeavour* linking Boston, Massachusetts, and Boston, Lincolnshire. In the picture opposite she is arriving in Massachusetts in August 1998. The picture on the right shows her sailing past Skirbeck church in 1997, photographed by David Hart on behalf of Addy's.

To mark *Endeavour*'s arrival in Massachusetts, Councillor Alan Day DFC (Mayor of Boston, Lincolnshire) went to meet his counterpart, Thomas Menino, famous for his 'Meninoisms'.

The market has always been a meeting place, which is how the town earned its title 'Capital of the Fens'. The market still attracts people from nearby villages and hamlets; it is still the venue for swapping gossip and keeping up to date with the latest news.

Boston has produced some well-known sporting figures such as Chris Woods, the ex-England goalkeeper, Karen Corr, snooker player, and Johnny Cuthbert, the boxer who kept the Mill Inn on Spilsby Road. It could be that this local netball team from Kirton Primary School could produce a future sporting star.

A lone fishing boat in the mud off London Road Quay in 1999 serves as a reminder of the fishing fleet that once moored here and used to sail up and down the Haven.

Even in the 1950s there was quite a flotilla of small boats which plied their way up and down this stretch of water, but this could not compare with 1894 when there were fifty-eight smacks fishing solely for mussels and employing 140 men.

121

In March 2000 the Princess Royal was back in Boston, this time opening the Len Medlock Voluntary Centre. With her are Len and Brenda Medlock, Mr and Mrs David Medlock and Peter Lawson, Chairman of the Boston Volunteer Centre Charity (right).

Sir Richard Body was MP for Boston from 1966 to 2001. Seen here several years before his retirement, with his wife Lady Marion, he was made an honorary freeman of the town in 2001 in recognition of his service. Behind him is his agent Charlie Vaughan.

Just as this book started with an emphasis on education, so it will end. Boston High numbers journalist Mary Riddell, who interviews the rich and famous for the tabloid press, among its old girls.

Boston Grammar's most notable old boy was William Stukeley (1687–1765), an antiquary who practised as a doctor in the town from 1710 to 1717. The Free Grammar School was endowed by a grant from Queen Mary in 1554. If Boston is to prosper in the twenty-first century it will be because of these pupils who will set the standards for others to follow.

Many American visitors seek this isolated memorial. It is a chunk of granite commemorating the Pilgrim Fathers on the banks of the Witham near Fishtoft. It says that near to this place in 1607 those later known as the Pilgrim Fathers set sail on their first attempt to find religious freedom. They were betrayed by the ship's captain and some of them imprisoned in the cells at the Guildhall (then the Town Hall).

Children enjoying the annual pantomime at Blackfriars, with the help of college students.

Acknowledgements

For their help in preparing this volume I am particularly indebted to Derek Addy, Gary Atkinson, David Bolland, the Boston Preservation Society, the *Boston Standard*, Pam Browne, John and Judy Cammack, Peter Dennis, Sue Jarnell, Lorraine North of Boston Borough Council, C.C. Pond of the House of Commons Library, James Sutcliffe and Jim Tryner, John Middleton, Richard Hutson, Bow Watkinson, Tony Anderson and RAF Hendon.

Boston has been known as many things, from a card game to a slow gliding dance. There is Boston ivy, the Boston crab, the Boston terrier and even a Boston garter. Here we see the *Bostonian* tug, not to be confused with the Henry James novel of the same name (*The Bostonians*), performing its usual reliable service.